Intermediate Wire Weaving

How to Create Wire Jewelry Without Splurging on Expensive Metals

Table of Contents

Introduction

There's nothing that satisfies the creativity bug quite like making handcrafted, tangible, beautiful items. Artistic outlets come in all shapes and sizes, but some offer more rewarding end results than others. Wire weaving is one such outlet.

Wire weaving is a jewelry-making technique that is used to create both charmingly simple and stunningly complex designs, and if you're reading this, then you've clearly fallen in love with the craft. As one of the oldest techniques for making jewelry still practiced to this day, there's a lot of information out there regarding which weaves to use, what projects to make, and the many variations of materials you can utilize in order to come up with your own unique pieces. It almost becomes overwhelming to sort it all out, especially once you're past the beginner stages. That's where *Intermediate Wire Weaving* comes in.

This guide offers step by step instructions that teach you more advanced weaves, including over-under, circular, and bezel wire, among others. You'll also be able to put your newfound knowledge of these weaves into practice with the projects laid out in Chapter 2. From brooch pins to ear cuffs, you'll discover a world of possibilities that will open up once you have a few weave patterns under your belt. This book will cover everything needed to successfully complete these projects, from the type of wire you need to the weaves you'll be using. If you're not familiar with what is considered to be the "beginner" weaves, I encourage you to pick up a book on beginner techniques or do some research and master the basics first. You'll understand the intermediate weaves and more difficult projects better if you have a firm grasp of the essential weaves that act as the foundation.

After you master the intermediate weaves found in this book and tackle a few projects, you'll more than likely want to take your creations to the next level by making them uniquely yours. Personalization will be discussed later on, along with common problems that you might encounter while wire weaving and how to solve them. Don't get discouraged if you find one of the projects or weaves to be more difficult than others. Mastery takes practice! There wouldn't be any fun in it if you were an expert from the get-go, would there be?

Additionally, in this book, you will learn about

cold connections - how to join two pieces of metal without using heat as with soldering and welding - and discover how to make your own findings.

There's a wealth of knowledge to be had in the following pages, and you'll be guided every step of the way. So roll up your sleeves, pull out your supplies, and keep reading to find out more about the art of intermediate wire weaving.

Chapter 1: Weaves

Let's jump right in and talk about the weaves you'll need to progress to the intermediate projects found in this book and those that can be discovered online. Each style discussed is classic and one that is used for many creations. They will serve you well as you continue to grow your skills and learn more about wire weaving. Since you'll be practicing to start out, you can use any wire material you'd like. Copper is generally best because it's easy to handle and relatively inexpensive. You don't have to worry too much about measurements just yet, either, since we're learning how to do these weaves and not making something that requires set lengths.

Circular Weave

Also known as "coiling", this technique is particularly useful when you're working with rounded pendants and other circular items that are typically difficult to design around. While wire wrapping is generally the most popular method for forming frames around center stones, circular weaving creates intricate and visually stunning patterns that enhance the look of the entire piece.

Tools and materials needed:

- Coiling Gizmo

- 1 spool of 28 gauge round dead soft wire for base coil (you won't use the whole spool, but it's best to have more than enough when using the Coiling Gizmo)

- 24 gauge round dead soft for inner wire, cut to 30 inches

- 1 spool of 20 gauge wire (again, you won't use all of it, but it's better to have excess than to cut it too short)

- Wire cutters

Steps:

There are two ways you can do coiling, but we're going to cover the simplest method, which requires a Coiling Gizmo. These are extremely useful and relatively inexpensive. They help you create uniform coils without having to do it all by hand, which means the finished product will look more polished and professional. If you prefer to coil by hand, then that's fine, too, of course; you can skip step one and go straight to step three if you'd rather not use a gizmo.

1. Using your Coiling Gizmo, coil the 28

gauge wire until you have a piece that's about 15 inches in length. This is the main coil that you'll be weaving around a base wire.

2. If you skipped step one, your coil should already have an inner wire, and you can proceed to step three. If you used the gizmo, you'll need to thread your 24 gauge wire through the coil. You'll want this wire to be about double the length of the coiled wire, so 30 inches should be enough.

3. Pull the 24 gauge wire through until you have about 1 ½ - 2 inches sticking out from one side of the coil. Next, take your 20 gauge wire and unwind a good long piece - about 12 inches should suffice to start with. Don't cut the wire because you'll need a lot more, but you'll want to have enough to work with without it getting tangled up in excess wire.

4. Start a few inches down the 20 gauge wire so you have something to grip while you're weaving, and begin wrapping the 1 ½ - 2-inch tail from your 24 gauge wire around the 20 gauge wire. You only need to wrap a few times to secure it. Once you

feel like it's secure enough, you can slide the coil up so it's flush against the 20 gauge wire.

5. Now comes the fun part. Take your 28 gauge coil and coil it around the 20 gauge wire, making sure each wrap is flush against the one before it. Keep coiling until you run out of the 28 gauge length, then take the remaining 24 gauge inner wire and wrap it around the 20 gauge a few times to secure it on that end. You can snip off the excess wire so that the lengths are equal on both ends (you should have a few inches of 20 gauge on each side). Pinch down the 24 gauge on either side so that it looks clean and polished with no wires sticking out at odd angles.

You can either stop here and use your finished coil on a project, or you can do one more coil using the 20 gauge wire and wrap it in between the 28 gauge coils so that it's sitting in the grooves. This is purely decorative and entirely optional.

Over-Over Weave

The next two weave styles are versatile in that

you can use as many base wires as you want. For the over-over weave, we'll stick with three wires for the purposes of this guide, but just know that you can adjust according to your needs and project requirements.

Tools and materials needed:

- Three 20 gauge base wires (or larger if you prefer), round and dead soft

- 28 gauge weaving wire (again, can be larger or smaller based on your preference), round and dead soft

- Wire cutters

Steps:

1. Cut your three base wires as long as you wish as your only purpose is to get the hang of the weave.

2. Cut a good long length of weaving wire - between 12 and 24 inches should be enough to start with.

3. Secure your weaving wire to the bottom base wire by wrapping around once, leaving a bit of a tail to hold onto as you continue weaving.

4. With the weaving wire underneath the

bottom base wire and pointing toward you, wrap it over the bottom two wires twice, making sure to slide each wrap down toward your fingers to remove any gaps.

5. Now, with the weaving wire under the middle base wire facing toward you, wrap it up over the middle and top wires twice.

6. The weaving wire will now be under all three wires facing toward you. Wrap it up over the bottom two wires again, over the top two, and continue until you're happy with the length or until you have run out of wire.

Keep in mind that you needn't only wrap the weaving wire twice; you can do it three times, five times, ten times, or as many times as you'd prefer. A simple variation such as this will give your pattern a unique look.

Over-Under Weave

Once again, you can use any number of base wires, but we'll teach you how to do this weave with six. This pattern seems complicated at first, but it's fairly straightforward and only requires that you keep track of whether you're going over or under.

Tools and materials needed:

- Six 20 gauge base wires (or larger/smaller), round and dead soft

- 28 gauge weaving wire (or larger/smaller), round and dead soft

- wire cutters

Steps:

1. Fan out your six base wires so that you have space to weave the wire in and out. There's a lot of movement to this weave, so you'll want to give yourself enough space to prevent getting tangled up.

2. Cut 12 to 24 inches of your weaving wire. Secure it by leaving a short tail for you to hold onto, and wrap it over the bottom wire.

3. Wrap your wire once around the bottom two wires going from bottom to top, ending with the wire over the top of and behind the second wire from the bottom (it might help to assign your wires numbers - bottom 1, then 2, and so on up

to your top wire, 6).

4. Wrap once around base wires 2 and 3, again going from bottom to top and ending behind the third wire. Then wrap around wires 3 and 4, then 4 and 5, and finally wires 5 and 6. End with your weaving wire behind all the wires facing toward you.

5. Bring your weaving wire to the front between wires 4 and 5 and wrap once around wire 5. Then bring the weaving wire to the front between wires 3 and 4 and wrap once around wire 4. Continue following this pattern for wires 3 and 2.

6. Once you've wrapped around wire 2, bring the weaving wire down behind wire 1 and wrap up and over the bottom two wires, just like in step three.

7. Repeat step three, wrapping wires 1 and 2, 2 and 3, 3 and 4, 4 and 5, and 5 and 6.

8. Repeat step five, wrapping one wire at a time as you make your way back down.

Keep going until you're happy with the length or until you run out of wire.

Bezel Wire Weave

There are a few different weaves you can use when you're making a frame, or bezel, for a pendant necklace. Some are very basic and simple, while others are more complex and involved. The one we're going to look at is a little more intricate and on the fancier side. It forms a very sturdy frame for large stones and offers a more interesting appearance than frames created using simple wire wrapping techniques. You'll have to adjust sizing based on your specific project, but for now, we'll just go through the basic how to. In the next chapter, we'll look at some uses for these weaves and get into the nitty-gritty of tools, materials, and sizing.

Tools and materials needed:

- Three 8-inch 20 gauge base wires of round and dead soft (longer or shorter is fine; you just want enough that you can get the hang of the pattern)

- 24 inches of 28 gauge weaving wire, round and dead soft

- Wire cutters

Steps:

1. Find roughly the center of your wires, and hold onto the bunch there, fanning out the wires on the side you'll be weaving.

2. Place your weaving wire between the bottom wire and the one just above it, holding onto a small section to secure it. Wrap it once around the bottom wire going from top to bottom. Your weaving wire should now be behind the base wires facing up toward the top ones.

3. Wrap your weaving wire between the top two wires, pull it down, and then repeat (from behind, bring the weaving wire to the front between the top two wires). This creates two wraps around the bottom two wires.

4. Next, wrap the top two wires by bringing your weaving wire up and over the top, and then between the bottom two wires.

5. Wrap the top wire once by going up over the top, and then bring the weaving wire to the back by going between the top two wires.

6. Wrap around the top two wires again

twice, and then wrap around the bottom two wires twice so that your weaving wire ends up in the front.

7. Make one wrap on the bottom wire as you did for the top, ending with the wire in the back and pointing down. Your pattern should look something like this so far, with the colon representing single loops:

   ||:||

   || ||: (2, 2, loop, 2, 2, loop)

8. Keep following the pattern: wrap bottom two twice, top two twice, single loop, top two twice, bottom two twice, and then loop.

There will be more steps when you're using this frame to actually make something, but for now, that's the gist of it.

Diagonal Wire Weave

When you need a simplistic but lovely design that's adaptable and can be made with as many or as few base wires as you want, a diagonal weave should be your go-to. We're going to show you how to create this pattern with two wires, but you can work up to four if you'd like.

Tools and materials needed:

- Two 8-inch 20 gauge base wires, round and dead soft or half hard

- 24 inches of 28 gauge weaving wire, round and dead soft

Steps:

1. As usual, take your two base wires and wrap your weaving wire over the bottom one to secure it. It should go front to back and end up behind the bottom wire pointing down.

2. Wrap your weaving wire over both base wires, going from the bottom to the top, then bring it between the wires and up around just the top wire.

3. Bring the weaving wire behind both wires, then pull it up and over the bottom wire, just like you did in step one. Then, wrap up and over both wires as in step two, and finish by wrapping over the top wire once.

4. Repeat the pattern: single wrap bottom, wrap both, single wrap top, and back to

bottom.

This is by no means an exhaustive list of intermediate weaves. There are many techniques out there, so it would be impossible to list them all. Many of these weaves also have different names associated with them, making it even more difficult to parse them out. But you don't need to worry about any of that. Just master these weaves, and learning each one along with the beginner knowledge you already possess will be enough to help you craft incredibly detailed and stunningly simple designs. To get started using these patterns firsthand, continue on to the next (and highly anticipated) chapter - projects!

Chapter 2: Projects

It's time to get to the good stuff. Putting your skills to good use is the most rewarding part of learning a new hobby. Wire weaving is great that way, because you get to wear or gift your finished product; Christmas and birthdays just got a whole lot easier.

All of the following projects utilize beginner weaves that you should already be familiar with as well as intermediate weaves that are covered in Chapter 1. In addition, they don't require any special tools or materials that are ridiculously expensive.

So, without further ado, let's get crafting.

Woven Bezel Pendant

Remember the bezel wire weave you just learned about in the previous chapter? Well, you already get to put it to good use.

Tools and materials needed:

- Wire cutters
- Flat or round nose pliers
- Bail making pliers

- 20 gauge copper wire, round and dead soft

- One spool 28 gauge copper weaving wire, round and dead soft

- Cabochon of the size and shape of your choosing

Steps:

1. To first figure out what length your 20 gauge base wires should be and how many you will need, take your cabochon and wrap enough wire around it so that it covers the perimeter - then triple that length. You want it to be long enough that you can use the excess length to secure the pendant and make a bail. You should also estimate how many wires you need based on the width of the sides of the cabochon. You'll generally need three or four. Once you have your measurements, cut your base wires.

2. Using the **bezel wire weave** described in Chapter 1, start in the middle of the base wires, and work your way up one side. Periodically check to make sure the frame isn't too long or larger than your stone; it needs to fit snugly or it will pop

out.

3. At three points of your weave, you'll make a large loop that will be used later to secure your cabochon. These points will be at the center of the side, bottom, and the other side center of the cabochon. Once you've woven to the first point, the center of the first side, ensure you're at a point where your weaving wire is at/over the top wire. After you've woven around the top two wires and are about to make your single loop around just the top wire, use two fingers and wrap the wire around them **while** you make your single loop. All you're trying to do is leave a little slack in the wire which you'll use later.

4. Keep following the bezel weave pattern until you reach your second point at the spot where the bottom center of the stone will be. Create another loop the same way you did in the previous step. Continue on and do the same loop on the other side center opposite the first loop. Make sure each loop is on the same base wire - (the top one).

5. Once you've woven to the correct length

(the perimeter of your cabochon), set your stone down on a flat surface so that you can more easily shape your frame around it. You need to place the frame around the stone so that the loops are facing outward. Press down and pat the frame down gently so it forms around the stone. At either end of the weave where your unwoven base wires show, squeeze those wires inward so that the ends closest to the weave shape around the top of your stone. Ensure the stone can't pop through the front of the frame. We'll take care of the back soon.

6. Now it's time to close your frame. Take the front two wires on either side of the front of your frame and cross them over each other where they go into the weave. You're essentially forming an X at the very top of your frame. Bend those wires toward the back, then cross them into an X again at the back top of the frame.

7. You should still have your weaving wire coming off one side of the frame. Don't cut that off the spool yet - you're going to need it. You should also now have four base wires (two on either end of the frame) since we bent two ends out of the

way. Using the same pattern we made the frame with, weave them together until you have a length that's long enough to bend around into a bail. End your weaving wire by wrapping it a few times around a single base wire, then cut it close to the base wire. Use pliers to pinch the tail down to the base wire so it's not sticking out.

8. Using bail making pliers (or your hand if you don't have any), bend the top weave over to form the standard bail shape.

9. It's now time to set the stone, so place your frame on a flat surface face down and set your cabochon in it. Take the wires you formed an X with and lay them so that they're forming an X over your stone. They don't have to be centered, but each wire should be near the loop that's on its respective side.

10. Take one of the loops that you made while weaving, flatten it out so it's no longer open, and wrap it around one of the X wires. Once you've wrapped the loop around a few times, you can cut it off and use your pliers to flatten it against the X wire. Do the same thing on the

other side with the second loop. Don't cut either of the wires forming the X.

11. Cross the wires again at the bottom of the pendant and, using pliers, thread the bottom loop over and under them, wrapping the same way you did with the side wires. This will be a little more difficult since the wires are closed, but with pliers, it shouldn't be too taxing. Once you've wrapped the bottom loop around the X wires a few times, cut it and flatten it like the others. You can now cut the X wires as well. Try to loop them and tuck them in on themselves so there aren't any ends poking out.

12. Secure the wires coming from the bail by wrapping them creatively around the X wires in any way you want. You don't want to just cut them, because they're holding your bail together. At least one set should attach somewhere on the back, but the other two can be cut short and tucked under or looped over on themselves to hide the ends.

You are all finished. You now have a gorgeous pendant to show off, put on a chain, or give to someone special.

Wire Woven Brooch Pin

Brooch pins are surprisingly simple to make and can be personalized in several different ways. You can even get creative with this design and add your own embellishments.

Tools and materials needed:

- Wire cutters

- Round nose pliers

- Needle file

- 8.5 inches of 18 gauge copper round half hard wire

- 45 inches of 20 gauge copper round dead soft wire

- 12.5 feet of 26 gauge copper round dead soft wire (you may need to use more or less, depending on embellishments)

- Center stone vertically drilled, about 32mm

- Liver of sulfur and paintbrush (optional)

Steps:

1. The first thing we're going to do is make and shape the brooch pin. In this

example, we'll shape it into a flower by making four petals, but you can use any shape you want. Take your 8.5-inch piece of 18 gauge wire and use your nose pliers to shape four rounded petals (or whatever design you want) on one end of the wire, leaving a nice long stem that will be the pin.

2. Take your needle file, and use it to sharpen the end of the pin. Rotate the pin as you file so the point is even. At this point, you can either add embellishments to the flower pin or move on to the bead frame.

3. For your base wires, you'll need three 12-inch pieces of 20 gauge wire. For your weaving wire, cut 45 inches of the 26 gauge wire.

4. Using either the **over-over** weave or the **diagonal** weave, start 4 inches from one end of the base wires and begin weaving. Follow your chosen pattern until you have about 4 inches of weave. If you have a center stone that's larger or smaller than the 32mm recommended, you may have to weave more or less. Once you have enough to wrap around the

perimeter, shape your frame around the stone, and ensure each woven end meets at the top of the bead above the pre-drilled hole.

5. Cut 9 inches of your 20 gauge wire and use it to string the center stone, then place your stone in your frame. You'll need to thread the 20 gauge wire through the bottom of your frame so that you can secure the center stone in a later step. Leave about 1 inch of the 20 gauge wire sticking out the bottom.

6. To close the top of your frame around the bead, pinch the base wires together around the wire that's going through your stone, and use your excess wrapping wire to wrap the whole bundle. Once you're done wrapping, tuck any excess tails into the frame or wrap.

7. The next step is optional and requires a small, 5mm bead. Separate the base wires from the center wire, and use the center wire to make a few more wraps around the one you did in step 6. When you have 2 inches of wire left to wrap, string a 5mm bead so that it's facing what will be the front. Finish wrapping, then

tuck in any excess wire.

8. Now we're going to use the base wires to make "wings" around the center stone. Separate them so you have three shaped into a wing on one side and three on the other. They should be spread out side to side rather than bunched up. Thread them through their respective sides of the frame, then down through the bottom of it. If you want to add beads or other embellishments to the wires sticking out from the bottom, feel free; otherwise, you can trim them and loop them around so they wrap against the frame.

9. Now we're going to weave the wings, and, again, you have your choice of pattern. You can use any technique discussed in Chapter 1, or you can choose to go with something else you're familiar with. Start from the top and weave until you get to the back where all the frame wires meet. Trim and tuck excess wire.

10. Repeat step 9 on the other wing.

11. If you want to add any embellishments from here, go for it; otherwise, take the pin you made in the first steps and slip it

through the wings behind the center stone, and you just made a brooch pin.

Braided Wire Woven Cuff Bracelet

Cuff bracelets are super easy to make, but the end result is amazing. This uses a braiding technique that's fairly beginner-level, but the use of nine base wires makes it a little more complex. Like the brooch pin, it's easily customizable; you can add beads, extra wire designs, or fancy swirls and loops - anything you want, really.

Tools and materials needed:

- 9 pieces of 10.5-inch 20 gauge round dead soft wire, either sterling silver or copper (though silver looks best with this design)

- Masking tape

- Round nose pliers

- Wire cutters

Steps:

1. Line up all nine strands of your wire and use your masking tape to hold them together on one end. Separate your wires

into groups of 5 and 4 by slightly bending one group to the side and the other group to the other side.

2. Hold your wires so that the masking tape end is facing toward you and the side with five wires is on the right. Starting with the outermost wire on the right side, weave it over two wires, then under two wires to bring it over to the other side. You should now have four wires where you had five, and five wires where you had four.

3. Once again, from the left side this time, take the outermost wire and weave it over two then under two. The two wires that have been braided should now form an X towards the bottom, and you should again have five wires on the side that originally had five and four on the other.

4. Keep following this pattern of weaving over two and under two. As you progress, you'll see the bracelet starting to form a nice design of roughly diamond-shaped spaces and rounded edges. Continue weaving until you have around two inches of wire left.

5. Now it's time to finish off the ends. Don't

worry if all your wire ends are different lengths. Trim the outermost wires on either side to about 1 inch, then coil them inward using your round nose pliers until they form a spiral. Curl it over the top edge of your design so that it holds the outer strands in place. Your outer wires should be coming from underneath the others, so if you curl them over they'll secure the sides of the bracelet. Try to make both spirals level with one another.

6. Curl the rest of your wires inward using spirals to secure the ends. You don't have to do them in any particular order, as long as they all are on the same side of the bracelet.

7. Once you've finished one side, remove the masking tape from the other side and splay out your wires. If your bracelet is too short to wrap comfortably around your wrist, continue your braid on the end that had the tape. If it's long enough, cut the wires to the same lengths you had on the other side and spiral them inward just as you did in steps 5 and 6.

Now, you're done. That wasn't so hard, was it? Once you get the hang of this design, you can add beads at various intervals along the braid or even on the ends of the spirals. Get creative, and see what you can come up with.

Wire Woven Filigree Earrings

The word "filigree" might make this sound more intimidating, but it's just a fancier style that gives your earrings a delicate, almost fantasy quality. You can make the whole thing wire and not add any beads to it, but for this project, we're going to tell you how to add a small accent crystal.

Tools and materials needed:

- 4 pieces of 7-inch 20 gauge copper round dead soft wire

- 1 spool of 26 or 28 gauge copper round dead soft wire

- Round nose pliers

- 2 small crystals or beads (5mm or smaller)

- Ear wires or extra wire to make your own

Steps:

1. Start about two inches from one end of

two your 20 gauge base wires. The weave we're going to use is a modified **bezel** weave. Instead of having single wraps on both the top and bottom wire, we're just going to single wrap the bottom. So, to start, wrap both wires twice, then the bottom wire **four times**. Then wrap both wires twice and the bottom wire four times. Your pattern should look something like this (dots represent single wraps):

||....||....||....||

2. Continue with the pattern until you have **eighteen** double wraps (||), then add **eight** single wraps to the bottom wire (........). The end weave should look like this: (||........).

3. Bend your top base wire into a tight loop so that it folds back on itself rather than forward, then realign it with the bottom base wire. The loop should be above the eight single wraps.

4. Continue on with your pattern, starting with two double wraps and four single wraps. Keep going until you have **five** double wraps, but this time don't add the four single wraps after the last double.

Instead, wrap around the top wire a few times to secure your weave.

5. Using the loop you created with the base wire as your topmost point, bend the frame you've made into a U shape. Now take the side that has the most weaves (the end you started with) and, starting at the 6th double wrap, bend that end upward to form an upside down U. The 6th double wrap should be the bottommost point.

6. On the end you started weaving, you should have a short tail left by your weaving wire. Wrap that around a few times to secure it, and then trim it and flatten it against the base wire.

7. You should now have two base wires pointing down and two pointing up. Bend your base wires inward so that they all point toward the finished side of the frame. Trim your wires so that the innermost ones touch the inside of the frame and the outermost wires reach slightly past the frame. Curl the outermost wires so that the ends form little spirals that fit within the frame. Do the same with the innermost wires, but

curl them a little tighter so that they're closer to the opposite side of the frame from the other spirals.

8. Your weaving wire should still be connected. If it isn't, you'll have to wrap a new one on. Either way, keep doing single loops (on one of the innermost wires forming a tight spiral) until you're about midway up the spiral.

9. At this point, you'll need to cut your weaving wire off the spool to make the next wrap easier. Thread the end of your weaving wire through the tight spiral so that it comes out of the back, then begin weaving around the outermost spiral that's behind the spiral you started with. Keep wrapping until your weaving wire has reached the point where the spiral touches the inner edge of the frame, then make two double wraps around both the frame and the outermost spiral to attach it. Next, return to making the single loops going around the spiral until you've reached about midway (this should only take four or five wraps). Trim and flatten/pinch down the wire.

10. To do the same on the other two spirals,

cut a long length of weaving wire and follow the same wrapping pattern you did in steps 8 and 9 with one modification - when you've woven the tighter spiral to the point where it almost touches the other tight spiral, weave once around the other spiral to connect the two, then continue your single wraps.

11. Before you reach the end of the longer outermost spiral, if you want to attach a crystal, get to about midway up the outermost wire then thread your bead onto your weaving wire. Once the crystal is in between the two sets of spirals (in the middle of your earring), wrap a couple of times around the outermost spiral you already wrapped in step 9 to secure the crystal and wire in place. Then, thread it through the bead again to bring your wire back to the unfinished spiral. Keep wrapping the outermost spiral in the same way as in step 9.

12. Repeat steps 1-11 to create the second earring. Attach ear wires to both, and then you are finished.

Wire Tree Pendant

Unquestionably, one of the most iconic symbols for jewelry is the tree of life. So, it only makes sense that you should learn how to work it into your wire weaving designs.

Tools and materials needed:

- 16 gauge copper round dead soft wire (length varies based on the stone being used)
- 1 spool of 26 gauge copper round dead soft wire
- 14 pieces of 24 gauge copper round dead soft wire, with each piece double the length of your center stone
- Large center stone; 2 inches is a good size to start with
- Wire cutters
- Round nose pliers
- Bezel making pliers
- Masking tape

Steps:

1. Cut a length of 16 gauge wire that's three

times the length of your center stone. Start shaping the wire around your stone by placing the bottom of your stone at the center of the wire and forming the wire around it. You should have roughly equal ends overlapping at the top of the stone, and you want the frame to be just a touch larger than your stone. Once you have the right size, bend your wires outward slightly at the top where they meet at the top of the stone. This marks your end points and where you will make the bail.

2. We're going to weave the bail first so that the frame stays in the correct shape. Make sure your base wires are separated by about a quarter of an inch or however wide you want your bail to be. Use the pattern of your choice for the bail - you can do a modified **bezel** weave, **diagonal** weave, modified **over-over**, or anything else you would like. Just as in the first project (pendant), weave until you have a long enough length that you can bend it over into a bail using your bail making pliers. Don't cut your excess wire coming from the bail just yet; you'll need them to secure the stone. Bend them into any shape that suits you, as long as it's in such a way that it will

prevent the stone from popping out. You can finish off the ends into spirals if you so desire. Just make sure they're touching the frame so you can secure them to it.

3. Now, it's time for the tree. Take your 14 pieces of 24 gauge wire and hold them in a bundle so the ends are aligned. Using your round nose pliers, start twisting about a third of the way down to form the roots and bottom of the trunk. Then take smaller sections of the wire on the other side (opposite the roots) and twist them to make branches. This is where you have the opportunity to get creative, because you can make your tree look any way you want. Occasionally, you should hold your tree up to the stone to see if you like the look. Don't twist all the way to the ends of the wire as you'll need some length to secure the tree to the frame.

4. The first part you want to attach is the roots. Take a nice big piece of masking tape and lay it on the back of your frame, and then set your stone in. You should have a couple long ends of tape on either side of the frame. Use these to secure your tree down, but don't get any tape on

the roots since you want to work with those.

5. Using your pliers, thread each individual root through the frame and wrap them around several times to secure them. If you made loops with the excess base wire in the back, don't forget to wrap some of the roots around those to secure them to the frame as well. When you're done, trim and tuck any root wires that are sticking out.

6. Now we're going to secure the branches. Fan them out into whatever arrangement you want, then attach the excess wire coming from the branches just as you did with the roots. Again, if your base wires are touching the frame in any place where you're securing branches, also wrap the wires around these to attach them to the frame as well. Trim and tuck the tails of any branch wires and make sure you're happy with the way the branches are arranged.

You are now done. That's all it takes to make a gorgeous and unique tree of life pendant.

Wire Woven Ring

This last project is incredibly customizable. You can use any weaving technique you want, and you will make a frame for a center stone to add on, finishing it up with some pretty spirals or really anything else.

Tools and materials needed:

- 2-3 pieces of 20 gauge copper round dead soft wire, cut to roughly 3.5 inches

- 3 feet of 28 gauge copper round dead soft wire

- Wire cutters

- Ring sizer (or just your own finger)

- Round nose pliers

Steps:

1. Starting with your 20 gauge base wires, begin wrapping the 28 gauge weaving wire in any pattern you want. The number of base wires you use depends on both the pattern you want and the width you'd like the ring to be. Feel free to exercise your creative freedom here.

2. Weave your chosen pattern until the

length is long enough to wrap around into your desired ring size. You'll want to periodically check to see how you're doing, because if you weave too much, your ring will be too big. Once you've woven the proper length, finish by wrapping the weaving wire a few more times, trim it, and flatten/pinch down the tail.

3. Shape the ring around your ring shaper or another object that's the right size. Try to secure it on tightly, because you'll need something to hold the ring steady as you finish the base wire ends.

4. This is another step where you can get creative. You'll have either four or six base wire ends coming from your weave, and to close your ring, you can make loops, spirals, twisted knots, and anything else you can think of. There are so many unique ways to finish this project, so let your imagination run wild!

That's it for the projects, but hopefully, these have inspired you to start creating your own designs. Play around with different weaves and stone sizes to make entirely new creations that are 100 percent your own.

[BONUS] Donut Bail Pendant

This is very simple work and thus requires simple skill. Because of its end product, which is a whole donut bail pendant, there will be a preparative work prior to the main job. In other words, this project is a beginner one but combines simple preparatory works with the main one. The preparation is expedient because without it the foundation will not be made for the huge job. In the same vein, the main job needs a pendant so, make sure the size and type of the pendant are determined too. Make sure you follow the steps swiftly even as you read.

The following are techniques needed to finish the job:

Weaving

Downhill single Flame Stitch

Wrapping

These techniques are very basic and must have been acquired from the beginning of this book if otherwise, make sure you revise the section that deals with techniques.

Materials:

33 in. 20-gauge dead-soft copper wire

3½ ft. 24-gauge dead-soft copper wire

50mm gemstone donut

10mm large-hole copper bead

3mm bead

40 80 seed beads

Daisy spacer with a large hole

Ruler

Chain nose pliers

Round nose pliers

The following are the things to get ready before going to the main work:

Step 1

Weave a bail for a donut-shaped stone with about a large 50mm jasper donut.

Step 2

Make sure that the weave is adjustable to fit any size

Step 3

Prepare the Downhill Single Flame Stitch technique for it would be needed at the woven section.

Step 4

You will need to learn if you have not mastered how to embellish with seed beads for a dash of color and texture.

To the main project now, make sure everything needed –the techniques, materials and the pre-working stages –is ready.

Then follow the step-by-step guide below:

Step 1

Making the base wire. For the base wire, pick a 20-gauge wire and cut six pieces of it. Drop this.

Step 2

Then, pick the 24-gauge wire and cut one piece of it for the weaving wire.

Step 3

At this stage, you will need to know how much wire needed for your base stone.

Step 4

Then, Wrap a cord or string through the stone.

Step 5

Make a mark for the overlap.

Step 6

Caution needs to be taken here make sure the measurement of this length is 2½ inches.

Step 7

To complete the overlapping, add 3 in. to that measurement of the length of the base wires.

Step 8

Make a cut of six 5½ in. pieces of wire.

Step 9

Pick up the base wire #6 at the top of the Weave.

Step 10

You will need to string a 60 seed bead about 1 in. from the end of base wire 6.

Step 11

Make sure that this spacer bead makes room in the weave to add more beads later.

Step 12

Pick the weaving wire, now, place it to the right of the bead and on top of the base wire. Make sure the placement is 1 in. from the end.

Step 13

Then, at the center where both wires (base and weaving) overlapped, hold it with your left thumb and index finger.

Step 14

With everything held in the right place and proportion, wrap the weaving wire three times to the right of the bead.

Step 15

You want to prepare the base wires for weaving. Do this by doing the Downhill Wire Preparation.

Step 16

For this Downhill wire preparation, make a single Wrap.

Step 17

On base wire #1, at the bottom of the weave, string a spacer seed bead, and then complete the last wrap of the Downhill Wire Preparation.

Step 18

Remove the two spacer beads to the left and slide them back on base wires #1 and #6 to the right of the weave.

Step 19

Bring the weaving wire from behind up two base wires and go between base wires #4 and #5.

Step 20

Note that this must put you at the top of the hill as you bring the weaving wire up, over, and straight down the back, making the jump behind the weave so you can repeat the downhill pattern.

Step 21

Begin Downhill Flame Stitch Weave single wrap. At the bottom of every hill, at base wire #1, string a seed bead on base wires #1 and #6.

Step 22

You will continue with Downhill Flame Stitch Weave, stringing seed beads on base wires #1 and #6 as you go.

Step 23

Don't panic if your stitches don't want to stay in neat i.e., like in the diagonal lines because you could pinch them with chain nose pliers to make them line up.

Step 24

Now, continue the Downhill Flame Stitch Weave for the length you originally measured with the cord.

Step 25

When the weaving is completed, slide each wire out individually until the weave is centered.

Step 26

Then, wrap the weaving wire three times around base wire #6 and trim the end tightly on the back.

Step 27

You will need to push the weave into the hole of the stone and center the stone.

Step 28

With this, make a U-shaped bend to fit the stone very well. Now, remove the stone.

Step 29

You must have noticed that there are several ends that need to be finished.

Step 30

Because of this, make a 90-degree bend inward with base wires #1 and #6. They should cross each other inside the weave.

Step 31

At this stage, end base wires #2, #4, and #5 straight down on the inside of the weave, over the top of the two crossed wires. Make sure you trim all the three wires to about 3⁄8 in.

Step 32

With the round nose pliers, curl the ends of the three wires over the crossed wires to lock them in place.

Step 33

Trim the two crossed wires close, up against base wires #2 and #5.

Step 34

Repeat steps 9–11 on the other side of the weave. Put the donut back in.

Step 35

Then, with chain nose pliers, pinch the two #3 base wires that are standing straight up.

Step 36

This will bring the two sides in, right up against each other for the next step.

Step 37

Make a double wrap around one of the #3 base wires. It doesn't matter which one, as long as it is tight.

Step 38

Trim the end and pinch it down.

Step 39

On the remaining base wire, string a spacer bead, a 10mm copper bead, and a 3mm bead.

Step 40

Make a Double-Wrapped Loop at the top of these beads. If you are adding a chain as you must have planned, connect the chain to the loop before you complete the wraps.

Your work is now ready. This is a very simple way of making stunning jewelry.

Making and Installing Clasps

When ending a piece of jewelry, most notably, bracelet, necklace, etc., the clasp is what hold the two ends together. A clasp connects both ends of the piece, allowing you to open and close the piece when putting it on or taking it off while complimenting its beauty. There are quite a number of clasps designs, and this is also subject to creativity and innovation. Many types of clasps are available in the market for purchase, but you make yours. To mention but a few, we have the loop clasps, S-clasp, etc.

In this book, we will be considering how to make a few clasps and also how to install them.

1. S-Clasp

Materials:

Wire- two pieces of 20 gauge wire of 3cm each

Round nose pliers

Mandrel- pen (this is optional)

Steps

    a. Measure and cut the stipulated amount of wire. Mark, using a marker, the 1/3 point of the wire both from ends and using a round nose plier, make a curve in the wire at each of this point to form an S shape.

b. With the tip of your round nose plier, make small loops at each ends facing outwards.

c. Now close one side tightly though cautiously. The open side serves as the clasps.

NOTE: To install this S-Clasp on a bracelet or necklace. Attach one side to one loop of the bracelet before closing it tightly. The other side will be left open, and this side gives ease of wearing.

2. The loop clasp

Materials:

Round nose plier

Wire of 5 or 6."

Steps

a. Pick the wire of 5 or 6" and use the round nose plier to bend one of the ends of the wire over to about 1.5" from the end

b. Then, make a loop by wrapping the wire ends around the pliers.

c. Then, to finish the wrapping process, hold the bottom of the pliers and complete it.

d. While making the loop, be very sure that the whole is very large to contain the hook you want to use.

e. Turn and bring the wire around and keep rolling the wire in order to make the loop center over the wire.

f. Hold the loop very well with the pliers and wrap the wire up to two to three times.

g. When the loop is fine in shape, clip close it.

h. Peradventure, the wraps are not close together and take the bent nose pliers and pinch everything up.

i. Turn the clipped end to face you, grab

and hold the wire above the wrap.

j. After the grab at length, bend it towards the back

k. At this point, you will need to make the loop like the time you started. Wrap down the first wrap.

l. Now you will need to make a clip very close to the first wrap that you've bent.

m. Then, squeeze smoothly so that the ends of the clip will join together.

This is the end of your clasp. Mind you, there are many things that can be attached to this clasp. In fact, earrings can fit in very well.

Chapter 3: Personalizing Projects

The only downside to using patterns is that they're not unique or personalized if you follow them to the letter. However, as you've just seen in the projects from the previous chapter, there are endless ways you can alter a pattern or add something to it to add your own touch of creativity. Here are some ways you can personalize cookie-cutter projects without getting too complicated:

Use a Different Weave Technique

As an intermediate weaver, you now have a good number of techniques under your belt. These techniques can be modified and adapted to suit any project you're working on. Many more advanced weavers even make up their own designs as they go. Don't ever feel restricted by the weave that's suggested. If it's purely for aesthetic reasons and isn't vital to the structural integrity of the piece, change away.

Add Beads/Change the Bead Size or Style

A few of the projects in Chapter 2 either included beads or mentioned that beads could be added. You can do this with nearly any project. If the project already calls for the use of beads, you don't have to use the same size or style bead as the instructions say. Use a smaller or larger center stone, add faceted beads instead of round, and make your pieces stand out even more by including beads where the pattern does not. Just make sure you first read through the instructions thoroughly to ensure any alterations you make won't affect a later aspect of the design.

Get Creative with Your Supplies

You may not always have all the materials on hand that you need for a project. Instead of rushing out to the nearest crafting store, see if you can make do with what you have on hand. Who knows, you may end up making something you like better than you first thought you would.

Also, remember that even if a certain wire material is specified, you don't necessarily have to use that kind. If you want to use copper instead of silver or silver instead of brass (and so on and so forth), that's up to you. It is recommended that you stick with the wire hardness that the pattern suggests, though, since that will directly affect the ease with which you can weave as well as the structure of the end result.

Chapter 4: Common Wire Weaving Problems

No art form is without its own unique difficulties. Wire weaving, in particular, poses a few challenges for beginners and experts alike. You don't have to stress about it, though. Others have come before you and paved the way so that your own journey would be easier.

Here are five of the most common problems or questions you might encounter while wire weaving and how to solve them.

What Are Some Inexpensive but Effective Wire Choices for First Timers/Intermediate Weavers?

Perhaps the most important decision you'll make about any project is the type of wire you use. Your wire choice defines the look and ease of the project, so it's best to be informed about all your options and have a few tried and tested options that you regularly turn to.

A surprising discovery made by many people just getting into wire weaving is that there are more wire options than expected. Some of the most common metals used in jewelry making are copper, aluminum, nickel, brass, sterling silver, and iron. Many metals can be made in different colors like the traditional gold and silver using filling and plating processes.

For beginner and intermediate weavers alike, copper is often the ideal choice. It's inexpensive and easy to work with, plus it makes beautiful designs and is readily available in a wide range of gauges.

Another option is pure or fine silver wire. It's less prone to breaking than sterling silver and thus is much easier (and less frustrating) to work with.

How Do I Stop Overworking and Mangling My Base Wires?

Your base wires are the framework of your weaving project and will either make your life easier or cause you endless headaches. Handling them takes practice, but there are a few things you can do to speed up the learning process.

1. Be sure you cut the right length for your project. Too short, and you'll be struggling to weave too much wire on

limited space; too long, and you'll have extra wire tripping you up and making you fumble around. Both scenarios lead to mangled base wires as you try to work around the lack or excess.

2. Relax your grip. When we're working with small tools and tiny wires, we have a tendency to tense up and hold our base wires like they're slippery eels. Switch to a firm but gentle grip that won't leave your hand tired and your wires bent out of shape.

3. Use the right gauge base wires. Most projects will call for 18 gauge, because this is an easy size to work with, and you can create many different weave patterns using it. If your base wires feel flimsy or soft, double check the gauge. Your problem could be as simple as mislabeled packaging or an unintentional switch.

How Can I Make Wire Weaving Easier on My Hands?

Jewelry making is a hands-on business. Your poor palms and chapped fingers will be begging for a break before too long if they haven't already; however, your solution doesn't have to be to stop and step away from the crafting table for a few days. On the contrary, if you stop working with your projects for too long, not only will you lose motivation, but you'll also find that it hurts more when you come back to it. Just as guitar players develop calluses from their guitar strings, you will develop jewelry maker calluses; wear them proudly.

Of course, you don't have to accept the pain. One option you can use if you want to avoid calluses or have painful ones already is to wrap your fingers in medical tape or bandages to prevent the wire from rubbing against your skin. You can also use lotion to soothe and soften your hands.

Aside from calluses, cramping and carpal tunnel are also problems that could develop when you work with thin wires and perform repetitive motions. One way to counter this is to take frequent breaks while you're working on a project to let your hands rest and try not to hold the wires in a vice grip. You can also perform hand and finger strengthening exercises - the rest of your body gets stronger when you work out, so why shouldn't your extremities?

Is There a Way to Oxidize Metal Without Liver of Sulfur?

If you don't already know, liver of sulfur is used to give an antique look to jewelry by oxidizing it, which means the metal is chemically combined with oxygen. It reacts with the metal in a way that causes it to take on a darkened appearance. What if you don't want to use chemicals, though? What if the smell of liver of sulfur makes you sick? It's not the most pleasant smell, after all.

There are other ways to oxidize metals. Here are a few:

1. You can use boiled eggs, surprisingly enough. Yes, it does sound disgusting, and no, this probably wouldn't be your first choice, but if you're ever in a pinch or want a cheaper way to add patina, boil a couple of eggs, crush them up in a bag with the shells, and let the metals you want oxidized sit in the bag with the mixture for as long as it takes to darken them to the stage you want.

2. You can also soak the metal in white vinegar along with hydrogen peroxide and salt, though in some cases hydrogen peroxide alone might be enough.

How and Where Can I Substitute Silver Wire with Copper Wire?

When you're learning a new weave or trying a new design for the first time, you'll more than likely choose copper as your material. However, when you're looking to gift your creations or even sell them, when is copper okay and when should silver be your first choice?

One big issue with copper is that if it oxidizes or you do it yourself to create an antique look, the patina or tarnish can rub off onto the skin of the wearer. This gives skin a green tinge, which can be disconcerting.

If you want to use copper wire in place of silver, keep in mind who will be wearing it, what part of the body the piece will be on, and if the majority of the piece is made from copper or just some of it. If you're making wire woven earrings, for example, the only part you need to worry about coming into contact with the skin is the ear wire. If the earring is copper but the wire is something like stainless steel, you should have no problem.

Chapter 5: How to Make Your Own Findings

Wire is good for more than just weaving! You can also use it to make your own findings. This not only saves money, but it allows you to make your designs even more unique. Wouldn't you like to be able to say your piece is 100 percent handmade, findings and all? While there are some findings you will want to buy just because they're intricate or difficult to make, there's no reason you can't start making the following right away.

Jump Rings

Jump rings are essential in various designs. While you can buy them from any craft store, why bother if you already have oodles of wire around?

The size of your jump rings and the gauge of wire you use will vary depending on the project, but to try your hand at it to see if you prefer making your own, follow these steps:

1. Using 18 gauge round copper wire, make coils with either a Coiling Gizmo (using a

thicker rod) or by wrapping the wire around something round that's the correct thickness for the rings you're making.

2. Using wire cutters, trim the ends of your coil so that they're even with the rest of the coil and aren't sticking out at odd angles. You want the cuts to be smooth, because if you look at most jump rings, the open ends are both flat so they can fit together easily.

3. Loosen the whole coil, then take your wire cutters and cut your first ring at the second coil in the spot where the end of the first coil is. This makes more sense once you have the coil in front of you. It's fairly simple to know where to cut to make the proper jump ring shape.

4. Cut all the coils in the same manner, and there you have it. You've made your own jump rings and can now experiment with different gauges and sizes.

Hook Clasps

Many handmade bracelets close with a hook clasp. Oftentimes, though, you can only get these in sets of two or three, and they're way more expensive than they should be. Both of those problems go away if you make your own.

1. Using 16 gauge round dead soft wire, cut about 2.75 inches off and use a jewelry file to smooth down both ends nicely.

2. Make a loop on one end of the wire using round nose pliers. Try to make the loop as wide as the widest part of your pliers.

3. At the other end of the wire, take about a quarter of an inch of the wire and bend it up at a 90-degree angle in the opposite direction of your curled loop.

4. Find the center of the wire between the loop and the 90-degree angle. Using your pliers, bend that the same direction you bent the angle to form a rectangle that has about a quarter-inch opening between the bent angle and the straight part of the wire. The rectangle and the loop should be on the opposite side.

This is a fairly simple hook clasp. Feel free to play around with it to come up with different methods and designs.

Ear Wires

There are so many different types of ear wires, but a few of the most popular are lever backs, french hooks, and kidney wires. All you need to make your own are pliers and a few inches of 20 gauge wire in the metal you like best. Keep in mind that copper can cause discoloration, so you may want to stick with sterling silver.

All you really need to do is bend the wire into the proper shape, which you can do by looking online to find a shape you like; you can also use a pair of your own earrings as a reference.

Which Pieces You Should Still Buy

As mentioned previously, there are some findings that take more work than they're worth, including the following:

- Crimps
- Pin backs
- Bead tips
- Crimp covers
- Bead caps

Thankfully, all of these supplies are relatively cheap and easy to find.

Chapter 6: Cold Connections

You know the image of the burly blacksmith hammering away at metals heated to astonishing temperatures and forging massive swords fit for warriors? It turns out that that's not the only way to connect two or more pieces of metal. While metalsmithing and forging are exciting hobbies, they're a little too much work for someone who's just getting into the art of jewelry making. If you're new to working with metals or don't have a lot of experience crafting, take your time to learn the processes that come before the more labor-intensive techniques.

To join pieces of metal, you can either use warm connections, such as soldering and welding, or you can use cold connections. We're going to focus on cold connections, but don't let the name fool you. Just because these methods don't involve heat doesn't mean that they aren't effective and durable.

There are two different types of cold connections: pierced and adhered. Both types incorporate a few different techniques which are explained in more detail below. One isn't necessarily better than the other. It all depends on the project you're working on, the tools available to you, and the look you want the finished product to have. Before you can decide, however, you need to know what each entails.

Pierced Cold Connections

Despite the name, pierced cold connections do not necessarily have to be pierced. There are two main techniques: riveting and wireworking. You should be very familiar with wireworking by now, because wire weaving is a type of wireworking. There are a few others that are discussed below, but first, we'll look at the different rivets and how to use them.

Riveting

Riveting may sound like a complicated process, but it's actually straightforward. If the piece you're working with already has holes or you plan to add holes, rivets are probably going to be your best bet. There are many different types of rivets including eyelets, semi-tubular, and nail-head, and they're separated into two categories: open rivets and solid rivets. The rivet you choose will depend on your project and personal preference. Open rivets typically feature a tube that allows for the use of jump rings and other connectors or wire, while solid rivets don't.

The tools you need may vary depending on the type of rivet you use, but in general, you will need the following:

- Riveting hammer

- File and/or wire cutters

- Bench block

- Drill set

If you don't want to purchase and try out a bunch of different rivets to decide which you like best, you can always go old school and use wire to make wire rivets. Since you're already learning wire weaving and are familiar with the various gauges and metals, this might be the best option to start out with, although it's a bit more labor-intensive. For this method, you'll need the tools listed above, plus the metals you want to join, along with wire that fits into the holes you already have drilled or intend to drill. The wire should fit snugly; this will be a solid rivet. Detailed instructions on how to make wire rivets can be found online, but here's a quick run-through:

1. Cut enough wire so that 0.5 to 1mm will be left on either side of the joined metal.

2. Make sure that your wire fits the holes

that you have drilled in your metal pieces and that the ends of the wire are flat and smoothed out. If they're uneven, your rivet will be messy and could have sharp edges.

3. Set the metal with the inserted wire on your bench block (steel is best). Using your riveting hammer, tap on the top of the wire on one side, then flip the piece over and do the same on the other side. You're trying to sandwich the metal between the flattened tops of the wire, so you'll probably have to repeat this process a few times to ensure the metals are tight together and that the wire is smooth and domed on either side.

It's as easy as that. Of course, the first few times you try this, it won't be so simple. Start out with cheap materials that you can practice with until you get your technique down. Alternatively, you can use nail-head rivets, which come with one side pre-hammered so that all you have to do is tap down the other side instead of both sides - but where's the fun in that?

Wireworking

As already mentioned, wire weaving is a type of wireworking because it involves the use of wire to create a solid item. Other methods of wireworking include wire wrapping and wire stitching. Since you're already familiar with wire weaving, we're going to take a closer look at the other two.

Wire wrapping is a very popular technique that is often used with stones to make beautiful and unique necklaces and earrings. It's similar to wire weaving, except it doesn't make use of base wires and typically involves a focal piece such as a gemstone or pendant. Basic wire wrapping starts with a frame that goes around the edges of the center stone being wrapped. To make the frame, you'll usually need the following items:

- 20 gauge square soft wire

- 22 gauge half-round hard wire

- Wire cutters

- Flat nose pliers

- Tape

- Felt tip pen

- Ruler

While some steps may vary from project to project, here is how a basic frame is made:

1. Cut six pieces of the 20 gauge wire measuring about 8 inches (though the length may vary depending on the center stone size). These are your main frame wires that will go around the perimeter of the stone.

2. Line up the six pieces side by side and tape them together at the ends. You want them all to be as even as possible, since in the next step you'll be binding them to create a solid frame.

3. Use your felt tip pen to draw a line through the center of the frame (this will be at about 4 inches). The line represents your first binding site.

4. Cut a 5-inch piece of the 22 gauge wire. This is your binding wire.

5. Wrap the binding wire around the center mark you made on the frame using your flat nose pliers. There should be equal lengths of binding on either side of the mark, and the wraps should be snug up against one another so no gaps show.

6. Measure out a quarter-inch from the edge of the binding on either side and then another quarter-inch from each of

those lines. In between the two lines you just drew on either side of the middle binding, you're going to repeat step 5. You should have a total of three bindings wrapped around the frame.

The steps can vary greatly from this point, but this should provide you with a place to start. From here, you can add your stone and let your imagination run wild as you design intricate loops and curls around the centerpiece and along the frame. There are endless ways to go from here, so play around with it and see what you can create.

Wire stitching is a lot more complex and is beyond the scope of this book, but there are many resources out there if you want to give it a try. It essentially involves joining rows of beads using stitch-like patterns, but with wire instead of thread.

Adhered Cold Connections

The name alone is fairly self-explanatory. Adhered cold connections make use of bonding materials to hold pieces of metal together. Don't underestimate the power of adhesion; jewelry-grade materials are made to be durable and stick to smaller surface areas. It's like soldering, only without heat. The two most common bonding materials used by jewelers are glue and clay.

Glue

This isn't your typical Elmer's glue that kids use to make macaroni art. Jewelry glue is tough, but it also allows you to create professional quality pieces because it's designed not to look tacky. With the right application techniques, no one will even be able to tell it's there.

Some tips for applying jeweler's glue include the following:

- Prepare your metal surfaces by sanding them so the glue has something to hold onto.

- A little goes a long way. Start off with less than you think you'll need and add more from there.

- Most glues need time to set, so ensure you have some sort of clamping mechanism to avoid having to manually hold the pieces together until you're sure they've adhered.

The three most popular (and effective) jewelry glue includes E-6000, Gorilla Glue, and Devcon

Epoxy. E-6000 is thick and flexible, and it's useful in that it doesn't dry immediately, meaning you can make adjustments after applying it so that it sets in just the way you want it to. Gorilla Glue takes several hours to dry and should only be used when you need an extra strong connection. Devcon Epoxy can be found in both 2 -minute and 30-minute set time formulas, but be careful with either one, because the materials will generally bind right away and will be more difficult to adjust than those with E-6000.

Clay

While there's no decorative element provided by glue, clay, on the other hand, can be used to not only create a cold connection, but also enhance the visual appeal of a piece. It can be especially effective if you're working with delicate metals with a very small surface area that is too difficult to glue. Kato Polyclay and Vitrium Clay are the standard choices, and both offer color options that expand the possibilities depending on how unique your pieces are. Vitrium Clay is also available translucent if you want to keep things simple.

One thing to keep in mind is that while Vitrium will air dry, Kato Polyclay needs to be baked in order to cure, so it's not a purely cold method of connection. On the plus side, you can use it for more than just adhering metals. There's a big market for handcrafted beads, and with polyclays, you can come up with your own designs.

Chapter 7: Suppliers and Resources

Nothing in this book would be possible without the right supplies and resources. If you're at an intermediate stage, you probably already have a cache of supplies, but it doesn't hurt to know where to shop in the future. It's an unfortunate truth that many local craft stores are far too expensive to sustain a hobby, and that's where online retailers come in. A few standout options have made a name for themselves in the jewelry-making world. If you don't already know about them, below we have detailed some places you should look into.

Rio Grande

If you talk to any wire weaver about where they get their supplies, they'll more than likely start waxing poetic about Rio Grande. Based out of New Mexico, Rio Grande offers chains, findings, packaging, organizers, tools, metals, and practically anything else you could possibly need to start any craft you wish. They've become dependable for their excellent prices and quality supplies.

MonsterSlayer

Also based out of New Mexico, MonsterSlayer has an incredibly vast inventory of not just wire, but every kind of jewelry supply need out there. Their website isn't the most user-friendly, but if you need an obscure metal or are looking for some really unique items, you should definitely take a look on MonsterSlayer's site.

Alibaba

You can't be in the jewelry world and not know about Alibaba. They offer bulk goods in every category, including jewelry supplies. The shipping times are a bit long (sometimes over a month), but the quality is surprisingly good and the prices are phenomenal. If you want a lot of supplies for the price of a few, Alibaba is your best bet.

Etsy

While Etsy is marketed as the place to find handmade goods, it also has excellent supply stores. Sure, the prices aren't the lowest, but if you need something fast or are looking for supplies that might not be sold elsewhere, it's worth looking on Etsy. Besides, if you one day decide you want to sell your wire woven creations, it helps to know the system and establish a relationship with a trusted supplier.

Leave a Review?

Throughout the process of writing this book, I have tried to put down as much value and knowledge for the reader as possible. Some things I knew some others I spent the time to research. I hope you found this book to be of benefit to you.

If you liked the book, would you consider leaving a review for it on Amazon? It would really help my book, and I would be grateful to you for letting other people know that you like it.

Yours Sincerely,

Amy Lange

Conclusion

Congratulations on getting to the end of *Intermediate Wire Weaving*! By now, you've learned a few new weaves, put those weaves to the test with some fun projects, discovered how to personalize future projects, and gained some knowledge about other jewelry making techniques that will help you make even more amazing creations in the future.

Don't worry if it didn't all make sense on the first go. Even though you're past the beginner stages, there's still a lot to learn, and it does get more difficult from here. Never give up, though. Above all else, wire weaving is supposed to be fun. If you're pressuring yourself to make perfect designs the first time, learn a new weave as fast as possible, or if you are generally turning the process into a chore, you'll lose interest before long. The best way to avoid this is to leave perfection out of the equation. Mistakes often lead to innovation, so don't be afraid to make a few; they might just turn into your best pieces.

From here, keep practicing the weaves from Chapter 1, and add some personalized touches to the projects in Chapter 2. There's a world of possibilities open to you now, so set out those wires, get some stones ready, roll up your sleeves, and just weave!

Metric Conversion Chart

Length Conversion Table of Common Length Units

	Milli meter (mm)	Centi mete r (cm)	Mete r (m)	Kilo meter (km)	Inch (in)	Foot/ feet (ft)	Yard (yd)
1 mill ime ter (m m)	1	0.1	0.001	0.00 0001	0.3937 00787 40157	0.00 3280 8398 9501 31	0.00 1093 6132 9833 77
1 cent ime ter (cm)	10	1	0.01	0.00 001	0.3937 00787 40157	0.03 2808 3989 50131	0.01 093 6132 9833 77
1 met er (m)	1000	100	1	0.001	39.370 07874 0157	3.280 8398 9501 31	1.09 3613 2983 377
1 kilo met er (km)	1000 000	1000 00	1000	1	39370. 07874 0157	3280. 8398 9501 31	1093 .613 2983 377
1 inch (in)	25.4	2.54	0.025 4	0.00 0025 4	1	0.08 3333 3333 3333 3	0.02 7777 7777 7777 8

1 foot / feet (ft)	304.8	30.48	0.3048	0.000304 8	12	1	0.33 3333 3333 3333
1 yard (yd)	914.4	91.44	0.9144	0.00 0914 4	36	3	1

Wire conversion Chart

Gauge	Inches	Millimeters
10	0.102	2.59
11	0.091	2.31
12	0.081	2.06
13	0.072	1.83
14	0.064	1.63
15	0.057	1.45
16	0.052	1.29
17	0.0045	1.14
18	0.04	1.02
19	0.0036	0.91
20	0.032	0.81
21	0.028	0.71
22	0.025	0.64
23	0.023	0.58
24	0.02	0.51
25	0.0179	0.455
26	0.0159	0.404
27	0.0142	0.361
28	0.0126	0.32
29	0.0113	0.287

30	0.01	0.25
31	0.0089	0.226
32	0.008	0.2
33	0.0071	0.18
34	0.0063	0.16
35	0.0056	0.142
36	0.005	0.13
37	0.0045	0.114
38	0.004	0.1

The conversation given here is strictly on the measurement used throughout the book. Apply your calculation using a calculator where necessary. Note that while measuring the wires, the centimeter and millimeter gauge of the wire could be used too with a ruler.

Resources

Anderson, J. (2010, June 08). Woven Wire
Ring Tutorial. Retrieved from
https://www.youtube.com/watch?v=iQ-
Az7jIeFA

Klingenberg, R. (n.d.). Easy Wire Hook Clasp
(Tutorial). Retrieved from
https://jewelrymakingjournal.com/easy-wire-
hook-clasp-tutorial/

Knaus, T. (n.d.). Wire-woven brooch.
Retrieved from
http://www.facetjewelry.com/metal-
wire/projects/2016/05/wire-woven-brooch

Making an Ear Wire. (n.d.). Retrieved from
https://www.fusionbeads.com/making-an-ear-
wire

OxanaCrafts. (2016, July 02). Framed Tree Of
Life Cabochon Pendant Wire Wrap Tutorial.
Retrieved from
https://www.youtube.com/watch?v=gfJPosJW
ikw

OxanaCrafts. (2016, May 20). Wire Wrap
Tutorial Filigree Crystal Earrings. Retrieved
from

https://www.youtube.com/watch?v=hindW3I
SnfU

OxanaCrafts. (2016, July 01). Wire Wrapped
Coiled Pendant Tutorial (Cabochon). Retrieved
from
https://www.youtube.com/watch?v=APb48z6
c9d0

Van Look, B. (n.d.). Jewelry-Making Articles.
Retrieved from
https://www.firemountaingems.com/resource
s/jewelry-making-articles/c12a